The Art of Anguish

The Art of Anguish

Thomas Sanfilip

Iliad Press

Chicago

Manufactured in the United States.

First paperbound edition

Iliad Press
P.O. Box 1202
Des Plaines, Illinois 60017-1202

Library of Congress Control Number: 2003110689

ISBN 0-9625306-1-1

The Art of Anguish

Beautiful arc of time
swallowing love: dance carefully with your tenderness,
kissing my hands
without color without remorse, o young hour
that poem we labor over simultaneously
forming this afternoon your body: that poem
that is waiting:
the waiting poem the melodic arches
of your thighs
before the broken hands of my logic.

The eyes of animals your instinct
prayer forgotten, snow forgotten . . . kissing
my hands without remorse,
o passionate hour that poem we labor over
simultaneously
forms this afternoon your body: that poem
pressed to mine
with your tenderness that kisses my hands
kisses without remorse
that poem we labor over this afternoon
the waiting poem of melodic songs.

Choral I

I.

A small reflection of sorrow,
or fragrance remembered,
like memory or age, a tender grip leads me
out of ignorance of night's true meaning.
I am full of its attrition.

Sometimes trapped by beauty and tenderness
buried quickly out of sight,
what they help to grow I observe & suffer for isolation,
singing fire to balance the stars,
to face life & night bringing forth rich symbolism
in a burnt echo of a world.

II.

You…
ineffable creature,
portion of conscience and semblance of self…
you by a blood in your dissolving grace,
I feel your unknown part rise
and live.

Inside a fruit out once the distilled center
shifts on axis…
the leaf pierces the branch,
the branch follows joy
bravely out of torment.

III.

Memory alone punishes the heart,
growing behind the lungs, engorged/blossomed,
sprouting a cleavage,
a child within, sunny beaches, lilacs, bitter joyful spring,
corpses of impression, shadows/contours,
yearning never spoken.

IV.

A memory transformed lifts its eyes.
Time intervenes its reach,
no more leaves to flutter
windy flags against my heart.

And memory of lovers,
hearts of obsidian,
not to resist the liquid of expression,
a myth of life and deaths.

V.

One more bright pleasure, blue, cool & windy.
No more mysteries promulgated out of mouth,
passing human figures,
a life momentarily created
spurts, jets and blossoms a watered seed.

Where is its echo?
What are its moments or substance unearthed
of knowledge and sense, decline and evolution,
words without mirror expressing a solitary voice,
a wilderness of industry?

To be complete to oneself,
radical to comprehend, a poetic reflection to your words.
I am their nutrition, banished & uprooted.

VI.

We are the night's separation,
its infidelity and insanity…
a simultaneously desired expression.

Every stroke of hand a page torn,
literature of tomorrow
equidistant from the center
of our last minutes.

VII.

This silence of heart is spacial, zoned,
street/dimensioned,
a disjunctive emblem of self,
pure and mad.

Seasons vaunted, endured . . .
a precious month: a descendant hour of patience
potential shouting crying patience,
a secret pain under the left arm…
pillowed, encased, sustaining life,
but ceaseless sound . . .
broken stifled cries.

VIII.

You...
in the heart, a sea my delirium,
a voice my history, sun never ceasing . . .
a dark banishment, the eye shouting a strong throat,
a voiceless frenzy of hope bearing gifts like an entourage.
There is no purer thing than you.

Out of impenetrable fervor,
out of love of all things I utter words so soft
this self would hum a blue vase, internal sky,
my sacrifice to language,
my inspired cry wind and frown.

IX.

A heart tumbles forward.
My hand catches it invisibly
the only assurance purchased breathing/alive…
the breast I touch, the heart I reach.
Nature sanctioned a mouth I kiss, flower of time & distance,
nose to nose, entrance I seek dolphins swim
up the current warmth we live.

I share the loin, humid & bright,
a throat and moan I steal no more . . .
naked struggling heart,
no backward glances,
no collar loosened to let the sun play over its edge,
no more quickly turning away yes before
a flower finds a sweaty palm.
When I am ready to look no more . . .
another phrase no more, no more . . .

Choral II

I.

Without conscience or futility,
one hand/one eye,
one circle, a silent year . . .
I fix the color of a purer night,
banished/consumed by my fragility.

It is joy and description,
another advancement . . .
my reassembled words purchased at a price,
again by dint of impulse and craving…
here to follow love with doggedness.

A season broke the vein.
A musculature is exposed.

II.

Months silent flung away…
deadness before life,
order and disorder I know earth by itself flesh,
drawn and pacified, molecule bird & fish. . .
therein my father and intelligence…
mutable, sea-protected, historical,
wind and parallel elements I will not let them part.
I pray a stated consciousness, a Florentine gesture.

III.

You . . .
beating centrally,
listening with an ear
against my chest to measure
the growth of your symbolism,
nights that release delicious murmurs.

You . .
characteristic of life beating centrally,
a heart's canyon, listening with an ear
cocked as though a pistol against my chest,
to hear the air grow,
night designating the beginning point,
undressed, remodeled.

IV.

Night.
All is stolen…
foundation tile & brick.

A waterspout falls.
Is it a question?…night is still a dry mouth
of words, overdrear & quiet,
a boat moored, a vein downward of the calf
downward reaching its own accord,
downward I do not question
words syllable penetrating.

V.

Now language is purer crested,
a nocturnal voice,
a foundation built and awakened,
freeing this form cooperative bounded by shadows,
death distant as fear.

The heart grows a plainer eye,
age making the father/mother dearer,
a reformed breath, alive reborn. . .
through canyons dusty and brave,
through air/clouds technological brilliance,
somethings endure…an earthless disenchantment,
a vaulted sky-blue porcelain wealth,
a bloodless arm without resistance,
childhood resprouted.

VI.

A quiet daylight peace quiet as virtue,
decade without diminished strength…
sweet contained final & philosophic,
against another in my kiss, my absolution by warmth.
I am comforted acknowledged reason can never explain,
a symbol outgrown the palm,
of all to live true being.

VII.

Pinned to the center,
hurtled forward like daylight,
I live with watchfulness & years
that slowly cut the threads of eyesight.

No matter how brief a return,
no matter space or human protest,
nothing mute in my voice,
still a tender word, a Renaissance
florid without imagery, anxious bursting light.

VIII.

Can it be we become opposite ourselves,
the hated self less evolved,
innocence neatly formalized into piled papers,
a theorized personal terror?

I suspect courage marries fear,
dumb creatures joined by horns the sea cry & doubt,
a slain voice, counterpart of my history,
the substance and hatred of our human indecision,
the perpetual study of motivation,
the catapult/fashioned human form.

Spare my peace here . . . moody abstractions.
Joy and sorrow are only words and weaker yet.

IX.

If I could by desire know verdancy mirrored by an age,
if this self-evolved poetic were as formed as art,
more virtue mine…
unusual power, an air to purify,
born pursuing passage, breathless & aware.

If one centers attention wholly on the self,
between bodies of densest blackness,
with intrepid color of observation,
leaves emerge.
We plunge the chest of the lover…
a sparrow's eternal flower without pain or maddened eye.

X.

The distemper of the lover's mouth frames miracles,
a noiseless individualism,
unwrecked, unbroken, borne overhead,
sad/fantastic stream confluent to my temperament . . .

The lover's mouth, a still poetic line,
dark as leaves, doubtful & meek,
adhered to a cry and gesture
which can never be eaten or breathed,
a blue and red palette borrowed from a dark imagination . . .

XI.

Unlocked, freed from trial, responsibility,
replete with darkness, inordinately black,
as though ships our hearts prows without repression
brave the maiden voyage,
with no dissimilarity, we stand to love the other.

We break with favoritism,
but the break rips open my heart,
blood/body stiffens . . .
still I hear yes inside a central beat/sutured vision
sprouting other forms,
nothing left to keep palpable the disappearance
but one short eternity of human experience.

XIII.

I measure years by embraces.
For each transition exists a point immovable,
a flower inextinguishable,
another language, fright & joy.

An hour of sunlight is the instrument of an idea,
a gesture taken absolved revered alone,
every standard our cry to life, to live within. . .
and the lover showers kisses,
and a gesture follows words.

Choral III

I.

Broken on the lip,
blue translucent/mud roar irresistibly fragrant,
the marrow of salt & earth
giving blood.

You listen at the navel of earth,
bringing eyes down, inspired and bituminous,
the pythian modern character filtering dreams,
deep suffering separation and mystery,
transmitting wing, transmitting character,
dead and living, my pythia escaped.

II.

Another headland pierces the sea,
terrain of lichens, sea-crab,
clinging shellfish,
heartless breakwater.

A roar returns a myth outside myths,
we and our absolute freedom…
sea-drawn, breathing to satisfaction,
wind of endless structure,
sea-broken voice washes recedes to its outline,
dispute crushed million/grain chemical sea,
you are what we ask
immensity, immensity…

III.

Fragile, immune to sunlight,
you could suffer,
but suffering does not measure us.

You construct a symbolism, lived and resurrected,
life hollowed out of the chest . . .
we forgotten, thrown together, separated again and again,
victims dulled to ourselves, a plead forced out the lungs.

IV.

Emptied of what no longer matters,
I come organized with a self-heritage,
a child's hands torn of romanticism,
a charted expression so full of heart empty of it.

Each segment a limb void of illness,
all else to grapple and rever,
escaping nihilism, pride, loneliness, physical and implicit,
to form no form of consciousness,
my aloneness, abundance of the positive.

V.

Can we in our nameless light
bear ourselves through turmoil?

Can we bury the shore,
locked together, fearless, with closed eyes?

Are the struggles, wounds, satisfactions
too much the love of secrecy,
so perpetual we cannot be free?

VI.

The sky cannot answer the memory of intuitions. . .
a woman of one excitement,
reimagining, rearranging our poverty.

Two emerge from the force of one having none
but one delirium that joins the oracle,
the reinvested mystery of woman,
mysteries dissolved.

VII.

The sea that grows in body answers you
from your sexuality…
lost word rejected, ancient word of form I am trying to speak
the torn wonder.

"No need to suffer, lover of other sound–name this yourself
from harsh understandings, pythia,
opened to full memories,
conscience meandering & covering the shoreline.
Name it name this nameless heart beating . . ."

VIII.

In a motion of extended reach,
beyond words, the unformed sentence,
living or dying through ourselves,
we live the object of our creation outside a rim of animation.

Wave-to-wave, a sea-glint silver fish,
I know better our two bodies,
creatures of metaphor… nothing of coldness, nothing forgotten,
death frightened, joy surprised.

IX.

The concept is you…a steel heart striving
over cheapened landscapes.

For the unknown digs at our eros,
love rejecting the concept of death,
pushing us to self-definition,
expressed in one word to another,
the word you were always thinking at the beginning . . .

X.

Having opened the dark,
spilling life/earth one on the other…one stone,
one finger caught pointing to the untouched syntax,
you find memories.

The best can live,
but as wings with no protection…
breathing air out the lungs, still as stone,
fragmented in my palm.

XI.

Everything, then spoken dark...
everything–repetitions following a path, a hand,
active verbs of strength & action.

The sun descends,
the night ascends, the day evolves,
everything spoken without imagery here more successful.

Everything & everything, bright young pythia,
lover, listener...I bend my ear bleeding you, filled with life,
the enigma of torment covering my mouth with love.

Elegies

I.

A nocturnal hour
shatters & splits into fragments.
The brief sound of passion
dissolves at the center of that low cloud, my heart,
hoisted into position, swaying to & fro.

The less poetic hour dances
over the seconds–winged creatures of mechanism
in the hour of breeding,
in the hour that sits above darkness,
the figure of my pagan rite.

Swiftly, the wind brushes the minutes
out of hand–gradually ever gradually they fade,
descending like sweet tears,
memories of yesterday whispering
the distant cry.

II.

Slight the sound of wind
breaking the thin figurine of life...the silence
and its plural notion of being leaving me grandiose thoughts,
languid lines of futile art.

Somewhere the fear, somewhere the naked voice
in the transitive stupidity of the moment,
other matters that dance blindly
up the column of art's destiny,
other frustrations tearing at tomorrow's portrait,
lifting the sculpted head to the light.

III.

The hour separates the wind from hand.
That last intellectual corner is turned
for some whirlwind of idealism.

Only sleep rarefies the system,
a turning hour of daylight covering the mouth,
piercing the eye's abstract perimeter of mind…to sleep
the waking fate, the muted torch,
the fragmented wheels of self pursuing yesterday's pale figures,
for all they say…the ambiguity of a Modigliani smile,
washing other shores of being.

IV.

Restless the dark
casting its soul to the sky,
a soft roar of clouds that swallows beauty & pain.

Tired I am,
this blue tangle of flesh,
motionless, a picture of questions,
but strangely purified I reach the empty space of thought,
of objectivity that turns me guiltily mystic again
in the stagnant air of morning,
waiting, speaking this bound word
in the wilderness of the world's being.

V.

In the somnolent grace of a painless word,
you hear me moving like
a trail of miracles
pressed against your cold cheek.

An air of burning light, like random stars,
pummel out of space,
forms the secret of you,
washing the pale veneer of silence from my face
in deranged colors of autumn
skidding slowly across the sky.

VI.

Slowly a thought scampers under autumn,
the separate evening
all but vanished.

No more presence of mind.
The pain under my right rib eases & echoes
the glib utterance of night,
dissolves the light rain that
falls over my disillusionment,
baring my angular chest like a dolphin's wing.

VII.

Pale pale echo of tomorrow
swallowing the wind....speak a thousand languages,
and draw close my burning flesh, my dream,
arcing another time over the horizon of sleep. . .

Pale pale wind
burning the trees in daylight...
turn back the cries of lovers as we speak,
for in half-closed eyes a Greek myth bears Aphrodite
to the sun.

VIII.

You hear the bitter trees remembering
the fecund memory of love
outside the sphere of knowledge,
the word of degenerated grace dancing away
before the public of my soul.

You hide for dawn…brilliant, though stagnant,
playing its sharp edges
against my half-closed eyes,
staring down at my bed, your figure in place,
your arm hooked under my thigh.

Take the buried roses,
take the fear that binds the blessedness of your lips,
for I see the worm of consciousness
playing with fate.

IX.

When winter's axis turns,
the misery of time indifferently moves forward.

Like ruins, the naked earth
is the invisible calm motion of violence.

Her sky bends as if a tired branch, an urgent darkness
making violent cries no one hears,
the spell of lover's eyes riveted on the horizon.

X.

Mid-afternoon fades
no nearer the technology of love,
only the geometry of winds
stripping trees of their meekest shapes.

I caught myself listening to the sun,
bleeding fourteen miracles
into the air.

XI.

My furious dialogue
is a distinct madness of moments,
setting your table with thoughts, like granite beauty,
fusing me to your happiness.

My arrogant chin
battles the metaphors of being,
favoring your soft touch,
nearer than the faintest moon
we dare the darkness of words, and always dark,
like benign lights crossing the faint line that separates
our bodies, good from evil.

With fearful expectation,
love's victory reignites love's sacrifice, speaking
its language, your frameless universe of patience,
my fragrant shadow of being,
knowing yet the final seconds will never arrive as we speak,
so love burns tragic melodies
I sing madly into you ear.

XII.

The old men talk,
making sounds that fit winter firmly into place.

While I stare languidly aloft my dream,
they ask what time.

But the drear count of minutes
interrupts the shivering night in my eyes,
paying optimism the price of obstinacy and grief.

XIII.

The barren hiss of late hours
moves the circle that holds the symbols
of chance.

Like a gentle aire of beauty,
each day thought arrives, like sleep,
waiting waiting somewhere in the anguish
of tomorrow.

XIV.

My lover knows
painful secrets, her cheek feverish & warm,
because there is no doubt with kisses
she begins her minutes with ours.

At the door
I tell her stairs are long linear fractions to solve,
my eyes in wonder, bewitchment & night.

Only her little boy knows,
running to the window,
tasting the snow with his eyes.

XV.

A faint flower fills my aorta
with peerless moments that breathe
on the hilltop of her kisses,
naked in the day, the sweet melody.

I was thinking with closed eyes,
like stark avenues we sleep,
sainted lovers of past meetings,
like a thousand dead summers, brilliant shadows,
not this hour, but the many pursued into daylight.

I walk madly tied to shifting fate,
the last sacrifice of morning,
with fear of silence, the loving gaze,
painful mistakes corrected, naked so the hour passes
as you walk, a blue arc of a smile,
hurrying to that sanctity of seconds
where our beings join.

XVI.

Winter
in its cruel pain
shaped the mirrored dream we started.

My fragrant misery vanished
the morning you kissed the poem off my mouth,
the morning you kissed the poem off my mouth,
a frightened winter in fragrant misery vanished,
shaping the mirror of our universe.

XVII.

On the snow,
a dark shadow dreaming a way out of oblivion.
Everytime I touch it with my eyes,
it vanishes like the sea.

The howling matter of the cold
begs the question from my lips,
frozen on the question of love that is no more,
or at least changed to fit the sanity of
the moment.

For each step it never turns,
and I cannot hear the murder of its voice.
I am its keeper of time,
so still the shadow eats the tearful nudity of night.

I watch
sacred seconds of winter divulge the everlasting,
grasping sweet words so echoed,
a shadow on the snow,
dark and still, drinking its essence with my eyes.

XVIII.

The empty wound sings,
crying with the last minute,
breaking like sleep my perfect tone…

Time in your hand
following the shores we mark,
my Goyan angel.

XIX.

I turn for home my paralyzed refrain,
spilling over snow, pulling the night to pieces. . .

Your soft good-night on my moody head,
a haunting present-tense in your eyes. . .
the tranquil memory of leaves
pressing your life
to mine.

XX.

The weakest link stirs painfully
the weakest touch,
waiting somewhere, crying beneath mischievous eyes
like languid drops of water.

One miracle of birth & death
waiting in the hand.

XXI.

Stiffly the wind breathes archaic beauty,
new beauty at work... silent clouds piercing the sun.
I watch morning shift cold
fragments of hope burning with power, my sanctuary,
as we twine miracles in place.

The necklace briefly thaws,
for drifting snow, plaintive skies sometimes have mercy,
the metaphysics of tears remaining braver facts,
shifting ever shifting the multiplicity of hope,
learning lessons as I shiver against
the backbone of my guitar.

XXII.

Now
between branches of heavy hours, no sooner
blink than all thoughts dance so calmly,
that memories live, that all hours must stop,
all gazes must, all gazes against
the blue twilight there…
only silence, only the color of fatigue
against the curtain
of her love.

XXIII.

We speak the silence
of bare pillows, like clouds detect the cruelty of tomorrow…
soft speaking, we dream plumes of smoke
drifting aimlessly.

O plumed one,
see the barely living presence of mankind in my eyes,
the mystical rite fixed in your smile,
love's imprint pacing the room as we sleep?

XIV.

I watch
technologic gods tracing paths in frigid air,
their lights, slow-moving on the wind. . .

Like open arms, bodies of light,
torso of lights…like strings of thought,
like wings of rectilinear grace,
so peacefully lamentedly stoic…

I memorize
their mercurial dance, the night's open arms
embrace embrace my futile months, this minute,
embrace & dying the scintillant night
of winter.

XXV.

What last word to seek
transforms the secret in pallid shadows…
tomorrow's sacrifice without forgetting
the tragedies we consume,
breathing in the snow this winter that binds
the only reality we are.

To it alone, remember the afternoon,
the painful immobility of destiny…
her breast dying of love,
sleeping forever this Sunday
rising in tearful echoes.

Oracles

I.

You are watching me
in the crown of pain fusing
these shadows,
this afternoon our static fruit,
& love burning the minutes & space between.

Those darkened
permutated clouds, the shadows
& your drawn expression
my eyes reveal
in the last refuge of reason,
dividing the world, my Latin prayer.

But still existent, the passion
of our slavery
that lights its being
across our night, looking to the violence
of divisiveness we endure
the corrupted phases of our lives.

II.

The grey corners of December
break the painful forms of human space…
grey wind & silence hurt the eyes, the sleep, a few minutes
waking the memory, playing cannibalistically within.

The grey sleeping with anticipation,
carrying the words that fall…
the cold touch that disappears into our unknown,
the night, the day & miasmic sky.

III.

Quietly,
the night has you forming its fragrant tendril,
falling in silent blue . . .the circle of silence
& light fades & pauses in the order
of the sky.

Empty the seeming reality of our eyes wakens,
freeing the dying in somnolence,
as the trees lilt forming words,
the wind's presence breaking the solstice
of our lives.

IV.

I can hardly see the disjointed hour of our memory
daring to move a word from my mouth . . .
hardly breaking the surface of your presence
containing your message,
barking between my fingers.

V.

Above us,
above the doorway a grey arch below which
we stand–two streams meeting
where two join the stream . . .

VI.

You're waiting for the sun to spill
the soldered eye from a grey-blue overhead,
balancing tranquilly between cornea & image,
the day becoming that dying shadow I told you about,
bearing doves that fall to mothers,
walking children, to blue estuaries of consciousness.

The grey-blue spins the finished product,
crying in the flesh…in the tears of sex,
& those lost the day never finds.

VII.

I found the sun falling night
around our tongues, muting electric speed & repressed,
all descending in the fire of your voice,
the cry death . . .

VIII.

The spirit of love exists discontent,
fighting the spiritual exercise of sex & indifference,
fighting our better or lesser selves.

We stand beneath the basin,
the distance regretting the equation lying in wait
in formless dimensions…
our sky's immovable realities dissolving
the souls of the world.

IX.

I could take your silence, bruise it, destroy it...
one breath, one true word on your lonely mouth
expecting obedience,
some fragment of a word . . .

X.

Finally silence
& the bridge, some animal sleeping,
my right ventricle knows,
ravaging the severance, the unknown voices,
& some vague movement that holds us all
steadily in place.

Finally,
the wind bracing,
the lie against our truth & watching,
if it stands the broken pieces,
leaving shadows the broken sun reassembles.

Finally,
the sleep defined, a mouth speaking,
& no word acute enough to center the fictions
summer decides is finally this.

XI.

This evening the face of lust leaves discontent,
waiting & waiting,
hugging the earth & moaning lust or hunger,
proverbial & pathetic.

A summer descends barely quiet,
but quiet nonetheless…
all eyes staring, first right, then left,
all calling contagious, but quiet because they have no idea
the evening they call becomes proverbial & pathetic.

This evening reveals no mystery to speak,
but speaking touches
what this duplicitous lust can touch,
until shallowed to one spot of stupidity & liberation,
in that spear of pain, the death
we feel . . .

XII.

Isn't the obvious futility never later in life, but now...
all the excruciating beauty you are,
like the first day,
the last futility now to feel love?

Are you watching, forgetting...it may be better to forget,
regretting this poetry of ideas, not image,
what you would say without dialogue,
the day our truth needed broken stanzas & feeling at the surface,
touching the depth,
& having answers that kept you breathing,
having touched desire & its paralysis,
our skies broken blue,
your hand probing skies difficult to reach,
love probing death with our bones,
& eternal dialogues fighting words, killing our skies,
no one understanding but us...but no one...
all too obvious, or not obvious enough to see
the sad blue fading falling
languidly alone?

XIII.

One drop, one tear on your shoulder
falling effusively like rain
over your fields,
hands splayed, head turned, profile & breath . . .

Like rain, one drop crying on your shoulder,
rolling burning riveting my gaze,
unable to cry, but crying nonetheless
over your body, your kiss, mouth to mine . . .
one drop following the reality of man.

XIV.

And the dark shaded misery breathes
against my neck the dire descent,
blood & flowers, a summer sun baking the mask,
fooling the surface of this being.

And the fear of that love waiting tomorrow
revokes & breaks the sun,
the wind perilous on my heights,
calmly dying on the surface of this being.

XV.

Only daylight muted,
& time liberating numbers
at some feverish crawl under shadows,
a half-light humid & perilous,
the next step decisive under shadows
behind the longest summer day…

Her kiss & all that vanishes…
one step & the forgotten under the shadows
calling one step back
my living voice . . .

The Poems

Part I

Ancestor

I compare us...
faces of inherent contrast.

Carefully, there is thought.
A sea beats on the inner ear,
shadow of dark, ancient patronage.

History/new conscience,
they are pages & wings, aviary souls...
I compare us.

Night

Day, wind, frankness of mind…
odd, broken pieces.

Nothing but night, hardened symbols, loveless breathing,
body, sleep, silent desolation.

No answer, sad gift…for sleep suffers gloom,
conquers the heart, last enduring comfort.

The Seagulls

Arcing,
with wings spread,
a dozen seagulls circle under sky.
I watch their movement…
clockwise, white of other shape transforming.

An early moon,
crystal-white, oversees their peace,
a whirlpool and barely flapping limbs,
the seagulls pour inland…the moon, a hearth,
reflecting my joy, wonder and limitation.

For brief seconds,
I throw a face skyward, dying to be reborn…
the motion, the arc, the mergant moon,
they move the seagulls who leave the sea,
bathing under an inland sky.

No voices,
the seagulls pass without breath,
but search a moon, a darkness, painted wings,
arcing, spinning my heart two and transfigured,
in silence, the intangible above disharmony
arcs the seagulls, a moon's earthlike sea.

The Shell

I carry a bitten shell hidden in my pocket,
like a mask,
to hear its spiny back rub the life
too pure for it to have remained
whole life itself. I am its life,
memory, and noun.

The song it sings purifies my thighs,
the season bringing forth its contained struggle
through the fingers,
the cracks and whiteness of a spongy center.

Sing the blue cloud twisted on your ocean,
sing and have me shout in return
to a square, silent street,
silent and unlimited,
shell that slaps my thigh, pouring out your gazes.

Sing, sweetest life-trawl into my hands without worry,
blow a horn from your empty lips
with uncensored candor,
when it showers only sunlight,
without memory of your discovery.

Out the air from your lungs, anxious thunder,
trace the edge of your shadow to nights I border
with pensive thought,
into ears that cannot hear the palace and architecture
of my body's irresolvable identity,
until I feel my heart fail and revive singing your peace,
the broken steps that led to you.

Transfigured

This my age unbearable of its tears,
I erase within my life, alone pursuing its aphrodisiac.
I bite its negative vein,
pour out a wealth of cellular configurations
of terror and wonder.

No use in repetitions,
new form is ageless and transfigured,
canyons and vessels taking one world to another,
to form not obscure, to feel not destroy in any manner,
no paradox mine mourning terrible lives.

A Silence

A silence he himself banishes returns,
a heart without mind,
a silence he himself banished.

The Unreflected

I reflect you eagerly…
pieces of a wish born brightened prayers,
the history of land lying between memories of the body,
a vehicle of you, my substance to enter and define
the unreflected playing off a sensation of our lives,
born on the moments of kisses,
born on the moments of our lives.

A Burning Center

His circular imagination is discovered,
a burnt flower at the edge of volcanoes,
symbols, the unexpected.

His isolation murmurs like a soft touch
his lover brings gently
over a burning center.

His constellation blinds him,
for hands compress it, arms envelope it,
his flamed center burnt on symbolism.

My Earth Watching

There eyesight bordered by grass,
I breathe it ten glances, mystical and bright.

A spear of sky,
this language outside physical boundaries.

Step by step, imperceptibly, the complete gesture,
my force of branches,
my earth watching imperceptibly.

Too Late

Too late the shadows grow,
bearing the night,
eminent and sweet as the lover's mouth.

Too rich to taste love, to know love
without dreariness,
I kiss the lips of each thing I love.

Rebirth

Patient at a task, dutiful to a life,
the sun that reaches spells the hour
of my efforts herculean,
in comparison to the sun, until rain soaks, hands construct,
blood revives the rebirth.

I too break on efforts.
I too with a mournful mouth of occasion dream the sun,
to have life for every patient effort.

The Nature of Memory

Among trees, wind & bells,
without formed conscience, I am reduced.

Fearless, the face of wind is the nature of memory,
the soil, hands & feet,
the flesh and earth and electricity of a forceful life.

The shadow across my chest,
a memorized kiss, doubt and strength,
the things lost to a mother's voice filling a placid city,
silence, anticipation, breaking the eyes I formed.

How Sweet the Civilized Rains

How sweet the civilized rains,
the cool, the brazen, the sea washing tendrils of land,
the air with its odors, mountains to city beneath its feet.

How sweet the broken chains of history,
the individual thrown against time,
like a wave against a passing heart.

How sweet and yet sad, a future proud as space,
and sad…a word, a love, a dream.

Self-Portrait

Born from urging for truths,
with joy submerged, bitter and angelic,
brings my heart to form a face without mask.

Like a Black Mark

Like a black mark, my hand is marred...
a voice, an ocean torn on hostility & light.

It's the wave placed squarely in the palm,
a somnolent waking for a paean,
carrying a hand to the wave burnt aground . . .

Separation

Tears dry in a wind blowing from the south,
a rain on the mouth of my separation.

Tears dry like wheat on a barren day,
leaving marks on my forehead.

Rain feeds miracles,
the inexperienced naivete of my brightness.

A Day Born

A day without suspension, with dreams attached,
mountains on plains, gestures between lovers…

A day with glory wedged between the sky and clouds,
bearing a face of obscurity,
urging a day born without wishes.

Nothing Else

Nothing else to flock to stone,
nothing but your conscience, hands and fruition brought to life.

Nothing but the symbol that lost your reverence,
the love that lost your kiss.

Nothing except redundancy, the sky, the tide, the city,
the civilization.

Nothing and the birth of emotion planted on your forehead.

Nothing aside from breathing tomorrow's wind, sunlight,
unities spoken in voids and gestures.

Nothing and more salvaged from a human heart.

Nothing but all life, all and nothing, with energy & exhilaration.

Nothing save this one point,
being content to know it, keeping this abstraction alive I know,
the pulse stops and becomes nothing but the answer.

Cities

In landscapes ushered into being,
out of cities, words burn.

Dawn again sleeps,
staggers forward to greet the palms & ordered faces…
they are the cities hurtled into me,
space and still greater space . . .the ideals, the symbols,
how in them there is a chance for life, the world and memory.

Broken, reassembled aspects of character,
hearts without blood, orderless and yearning,
shadow tenements, compromises, order beyond
the cities of my vision, strained, made into what was…
they leave me–the cities remain.

How in the path of one darkness,
how in the unburdening there is such freedom,
yet the cities of my conjuration escape to find only outlines of
what exists…hearts like new continents,
vanished, born again to be lost again again found.

The Waves

The waves continue inhabit the roar.
We break the difference of wind, the ceaseless unending word
that bends, discovering what we suspect–the young escape aging,
the waves penetrate resistlessly.

In broken, lonely courage, reuniting symbol
in the aged and young, we insurrect for minerals, devouring,
reexhibiting.

The waves the sun inspires reject and continue.
We brave them–they taste our rebellion, create the form of our
courage without knowledge or method.

Are they done?
Are their differences transformed, their silence necessary?
In the face of incongruities, do we understand the order of our-
selves, of existence again?

The waves bearing an abstract beauty synchronize
the modern heart, tearing away the cacophony to the reality
behind, the motion of our readiness we cannot hear,
but act the waves in their perpetuity.

Idealism

The leaves cannot breathe hearts
that never touch.

A body yearns for seasons of idealism,
without drawing closer or forced out ourselves,
even summers die winters I cannot face.

Two Bodies

Reduced to sublimity,
we prosper, white & drawn…
two bodies in shadow with linen,
two numbers against the logic of kisses.

Dangers join,
logic destroyed, heads turn shaping darkness,
the unlearned act the truer.

You forget, and remember forgetting who we touch,
roaming other shores of self-creation,
we live, we die, a moon ever deeper,
rising to orbit.

Humanity

You asked with silence,
the silence could not speak the age of humanity,
seeds, boundless reserve…

Woman

Only the melody of your shoulders
to brace against the shallow stone of my chin…
the crevice between neck & collarbone, perhaps frightened
to be touched.

Only your shoulders know the statuesque stone,
leaves crying for cultivation.

Only a woman with sensual weakness knows what love bears,
when eyes seize it close, shoulders signify
the inexpressible giving wetting the mouth,
calling, willing sensation.

Only when they support, or bend wind-encompassed,
their presence excites,
their fever keeping undiminished the lover
as he lowers his head.

Only you must guide, dying or living on their slopes,
shoulder-to-shoulder,
carrying the body's desire, a living, slender tree,
eight-thousand years summoned in their mystery.

Aperture

The walls contain mirrors,
the mirrors reflect windows,
the windows guide away to a shallow distance
of the heart.

If the Kiss Exists

In the hollow portion of the heart,
the flesh joins tightly to suffocate our abstractions.

As the skin stretches tighter,
making blue veins visible, it's heard . . .
fractured voices, forbearances, a field plowed under.

If the kiss exists, if the heart understands our otherness,
the kiss is bare enough…placed exactly on the mouth,
we bleed forgotten pain,
and find strength.

If Sacrifice be Unconscious

If sacrifice be unconscious,
love bears fruit singing without a voice,
the heart lived loses,
and becomes itself.

Answering

Somewhere the ocean reflects away
the trivial remains of age,
forgetting the hard, almost clear point.

Inescapable are the arms,
barriers to the buried truth under the tongue,
leaving us pale as night embraces day.

If only one could hear the earth
grind its ribs when the universe is answering.

Immunities

The stripped-down nakedness reinforced
without equilibrium.

The heart...nothing laid beside its abstraction,
for without confusion,
hands grope in the dark forever,
hair &·hands urging on a transfixed sexuality.

But the dark beating inward heart fusing,
inverted to a mirror,
remembers the brave immunities.

Nude

Nothing left to burn,
nothing to reconcile love with nature.

Alone…endless, fought against,
alone with harsh psychologies, art, the numb stare,
no weapons for the lover to resurrect.
when grass freezes, trees torch ashes & inspiration.

Can we be there waiting to gain the familiar idea
of what life is capable?

Everything erected without matter,
giving what the hand cannot find
in the architectural fecundity of another word.

Evolution

That perfect, augmented line of an avenue,
pampered by steel structures,
binds sunlight,
radiates scorn,
searching the inescapable fruition of an empty idea,
arches & splits the eyesight matter predicts.

The sun has no conscience,
having hardly the space between extremes,
each line imitating the curve for all existence,
the unrestrained ego born illuminating.

The architect who points his finger learned his caresses
at the farthest extreme of precision,
but when the frieze disappears,
the answer still remains only concrete & filament…
not flesh, but a figure in material outline,
an idea meant to live in a proposition of brightness.

II.

If there is one fierce blossom left, and silence,
inchoate with decision, living and otherwise…

If the timepiece that measures the circumference of beauty
is really lost, we are no better a fragment of evolution,
only a biology of right angles, mid-morning,
falling from drear constructions.

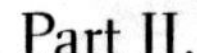

Part II.

Error in Judgement

Our fruitless energies
polarize with our last kiss…the transport,
the sunlight, a blue miracle in the enigmic face.

My hand opened an inspired shadow,
the miracle of self found land & suspicion,
the face is still dark…one instant without words,
order or philosophy or earth,
forcing the face to another mirror,
salvaging the monstrosity of our misconceptions.

Dissolved and diluted, the sky evolves,
but the hand loses its reason for being…
an error in judgement, we find ourselves again.

Radical Changes

Sick with emptiness,
the sky reaches down with a void
to sever my jugular...filled, empty, indifferent,
shocked at our sudden surprise.

Perhaps leading us to radical changes,
correcting what appears uncorrectable faces,
loveless, addicted to extremes,
a disaster of trust.

Irony

The day that counts wealth
buys my existence on impure coin.

Did we understand expectation,
armed futurity, purified action,
all that was ever purged at the sternum of the chest…
our ligaments of wire, the strong intention?

The long awaited becomes expended
and powerless, except the irony of desire…
therein, system, beam & radar,
unappeasable industry.

Orozco Draws

With diminishing lines of silence,
etches lift themselves with frustration & eyesight…
etches which happen to fall into view,
threads of line forgotten without purpose,
with every infused artistic line bending its heärt,
or ourselves washed away, slow reaching, in lost manner
our inert cynicism?…

The fear to avoid in drawings that suffer & explore
life with rings through its soul,
betrayed by the imagination.

Inequities

My expression is worthless,
and the solar plexus cooperates obediently,
struggling through exercises before I am alive
to truly reject or accept the world, or the argument
at two o'clock in the morning...
concerned with that friction which leaves me more dead
than alive, speaking broad whispers to memories,
to a future wiped clean of responsibilities,
finding inequities in words,
then realities once loved as one.

Cognizant Desire

I like a woman's passive eagerness,
quiet, without answering, acquiescent again,
speaking to the plurality of taunt muscle,
the male body.

I wait believing what never exists,
her fear of surrender…full, then empty, the face I thought
familiar, overcome with remorse…
all kisses that glance off my face, all darkness fused,
she stumbling into view, vulgar & seraphic,
body tightly pressed inward.

Like a repeated phrase,
measuring shadows & origins,
she endows herself, a question of cognizant desire.

The Fervent Explanation Within

As you made your mark,
the season shattered us with grace & silence,
indifferent blood...because there is no perfect age.
I knew looking in your eyes.

Should I find my lost self speaking quietly in transition,
the self expertly removed,
matter transforming the senses, otherwise free,
no fear...the fervent explanation within.

A Difficult Malaise

No brilliant effusions of passed conversations,
we learned susceptibilities,
picking fragments of character one-by-one
away from our eyebrows…

The oneness we could not retain,
the body I keep vigil…soft sleep, empty habit,
weighted into a difficult malaise.

New Language

A misshapen word is caught in my throat,
a new one born every instant…

The earth of my silence,
some awful sphere of rational madness,
surfeit & brilliant recognition.

Prefaces

Days progress,
detected & gradually lost.

For loss of minutes, the sun develops sterility…
the impossibility of afterwards,
the stupidity of prefaces.

Mistaken Inspiration

This fruitless earth, mineral decay...
a mistaken inspiration not truly ours.

We suffer like the unrecognized secret,
in feared silence, the terrible, somnolent dance.

Metanoia

An irrational form escaped and falsified us,
life sinking irrevocably into the last sin...
indifference.

I stood torn by memory...
the snow above your head in the echo of pain,
watching my secret dissolution.

Gravida

The answer like a frightened dawn
is a bland element resting miserably in conscience.

Only a single word from my throat,
a final thought of a selfless reality.

Ex Nihilo

Spring bears without license the changing poles,
clouds carrying the heart's transition,
existence against the answer to solve...
alienation.

Synesthesia

My heart contains itself outward in an outward love's
lost dimension, losing nothing,
leaving us again and again, like beauty lost in sunlight,
watching its last cycle of sterility.

The fraction of my substance,
worry of my transformation, tree to light, and substance again,
against all…to feel a last tension of heart.

Metaphysics

I am fasting
because my ideals suffer,
knowing the brittle quality of love,
believing in the existence of other words.

To resist is to forget the certainty
we do not understand.

Part III.

Samadhi

For nights,
the air chatters in a warm bath
of insect reminiscent sound of human breathing,
sweeping the last time table away from my feet,
as step-by-step I walk gently into the living room
of the forgotten word, forgotten kiss.

It is the half discerned face,
the image of a sun-drenched street
where money is a poor fragment of painless awakening
I walk…now a vague shape
over my bed of leaves & thoughts,
shrouding my mantle of peace in fearful circles of promise,
a near mystic figure against a background of waves.

And you, silent, dynamic, changed self,
confidently press the pain into manageable forms,
into lovers who no longer remember,
into tomorrow with its optimism,
& all else that trails behind these dull days of refuge,
touching my head as they pass.

Morning

The sky changes color by morning,
summer leaning leisurely from my window,
the pain finally subsiding like a wave of resolve
I toss belligerently into the face of tomorrow...
that leaning sky disturbing the tranquility of muted voices.

I, a fragrant ship, pursuing fragrant tomorrows,
selecting delicacies from the miasma of summer's end...
to speak and know the bane of feeling,
too late to say where the path ends or begins,
or uncovers the plural face of being waiting to be born.

Again, I swallow its formless dessert
of contemplation, a child of unknown distances,
sleeping destiny in a closed fist.

Evening

To live near dark is to breathe,
to wait the summer through singing a chorus of words.

Each aging tree spells the touch we feel,
each distant mental leap, like knowledge of a kiss,
takes us from ourselves to find other means,
guiding a hundred years of idealism into oblivion,
one word struggling free.

We undress saying nothing,
feeding the reservoir of being as the grass weeps silence,
at five an avenue revealing the formless secret of humanity,
inching forth between love & the puerile core of night.

Nothing but animality, a guise of humanness,
a rancid air of dusk
seeking the dim purity of thought etched perfectly
in the shadows of my eyes.
Perhaps not you who draws away,
but clouds the wind forces to disperse in pale light.

Spring

The cold wind
feels the mordant flower of my consciousness,
reaching through air to nothing but space & fatigue,
killing my sensibility.

The beautiful terror of love holds itself
to my cheek again, then vanishes
when the coldest touch of spring freezes my chest.

Touch its voice & time scars
the beauty of transition, the air living, the sky
shivering in one breath,
meeting the season in expectation.

Dialogue

I record conversations, my spectrum of interests,
into machines, carrying two voices
into artificial infinities,
between silences of plastic magnetism,
a voice which every so often shouts a passing sentence,
our dialogue on paper, the symbols breathing
rectitude of mind.

Now the turned up edges of history are loose,
tracing the invisible reflection of men,
with words, voices, the magnetic beauty of the voice,
purposeless, yet meaningful,
without volume or concentration,
playing the finite to prove the infinite,
when only to feel, to sense is enough.

Slowly perhaps matters resolve,
the imprint the same, surer realities beyond
a voiceless word.

Prelude

I.

This silence,
this pillow sleeping on its side,
waiting for my head,
this unusually warm evening bathing in peculiarity,
is too quietly sure of tomorrow,
my heart no longer beating fatalistically,
one breath enough to satisfy the inevitable.

My footsteps
mesmerize the idealist in my throat, begging survival,
but slowly toward sleep I walk, eyes in place,
spilling secret ambitions to the floor,
half-open windows allowing human tears to escape.

II.

I see miseries
playing in the dark, lovers filling space between dinners,
languidly aware of life,
a string of calculations nailed to the forehead,
a plethora of mistakes & self-delusions pining at the ground.

The prayers of trees & sunlight dim like lamps in sleep,
like gods no longer living or blessed,
sanctuaries of tired eyes
leading to the unpredictable minute.

III.

This sun craves the miracle of my humanness,
within the light of paralyzed mornings
the repeated miracle always in view...
see how it frays the lips of passersby,
the mountainous future of my love,
my lover's beautiful eyes?...

And if it dies the miracle in place, then sleep the hand
one inch away, the hand,
the revived miracle, receptacle of this sunlight,
o miracle repeated, this beautiful offering,
my half-open mouth puts to your ear,
waking this burning earth, my life,
in miracles carved passionately from my throat.

IV.

I am tasting leaves,
holding leaves, dying of summer,
a fervid hour dying strangely, falling from leaves
dying strangely above my head, a blind whisper,
rustling muted on old men's lips,
dying on the hour, the softest winds, the weight of winds,
keeping the sky intact, lifting the empty dice of tears,
waiting on the answer.

Now I know what matters,
morning bless the grass, the vigorous surviving,
a dying urban setting,
lie myself asleep to every costly breeze falling
in bright miracles, the open window framed in sunlight.

Season

I.

Now here, now there,
the season, grey then shifting yellow,
now the sky's incense yellow against blue,
leaves hardly dead hardly living,
beating my aortal symphony into doubt.

With a ripple of painful light,
autumn plays dank afflictions against the mouth,
separating yellow from grey,
the distant balance,
the line of demarcation, some sanctity of purpose lost.

II.

Tranquil, living grey dimensions pierce & plummet
the season's shadow,
breathing images of calm, side-by-side,
until obscurity becomes the countenance
in swimming shadows of broken light.

But too late,
all shifting grey dimensions weigh the possibilities,
the grim surface tightly woven,
now yellow, now grey, the season but arrived & inexplicable,
dying & becoming transition without denial,
the measure of radical turns.

White

Snow
against skies painted grey,
artifacts of being begging words,
evictions of conscience, broken serenities,
the morning moves.

There fighting
the white burning flagrant dying mid-day,
more definite the snow the snow inured
against skies painted grey.

And silence
breathes there the frigid air of doubt,
the softened hour waiting, holding firm
the bridge.

There, in purity waiting,
fighting the white, holding firm the snow
in spiritual calm, burning white our frailties
into night.

Apolytrosis

I.

I am thinking at forty-degree angles
the morning uncovers,
with its tentacle of minutes between me & tomorrow,
a million voices to come sifting out
the fuel of lies in our mouths.

My hand touches
the inner voice of things, embryonic morning alone,
gazing at my crack of sky,
crying at seven degrees below zero,
crying crying…holding its position bearing east,
too early to be too late.

By now,
it plays fiercely enough to soothe the trees,
aged & grey, in the palm of snow,
speaking tranquil symbols, tranquil minutes,
the living hours of refuge pass,
repeating eternal verities,
dying so effortlessly in movements of sunlight,
my profile cast, my thoughts divulged,
sailing calmly the wind.

II.

I turn,
breaking refractions of light
on a frozen miracle, a barren imagistic face
following the wind off-shore,
the sky chasing cloudless refuges into desolation,
and ice burning muted songs on my lips,
cutting sheaves of water ending in eternity & watching.

That great distance without censorship
comes fragrantly
on the cloud that breathes its freedom & silence,
the earth calling my dissonant minutes,
the minutes beneath my oracular lobe,
like addictive bacchae.

III.

I imagine
blinding light at summer's end,
balancing frozen against my next step…
the sky bent grey over the river life,
coursing a passage straight to darkness,
turning the mirror at last
to skies bearing east.

A blue effluvia overhead,
I practice the branches of death,
playing with my diction, the sound of my voice so blue…
my image dissolving, pounding eight feet
below the surface, languishing like loose dreams,
in the body's magic, my figure held serenely in place,
lying prone, close-eyed,
the sky cracking my eyelids between its teeth,
beating out, in even time, daylight arching slowly
into night.

IV.

I burn formless in obscurity,
the light diffused & stationary…the light diffused
& dissolving there among the blazing grass,
light & leaves rising alone, dying among our fictions,
descending in the cry.

A creeping blue edge of sky, half-discernable,
carries its burden,
rising softly in my throat, the painful order of things,
the sun's transparency fixing the sky in sacramental rays
of geometric line, immobile shadows
yielding the minute.

Carefully,
in fuming thoughts, like seas of metaphysical rain,
the light burns bearing slightly left,
wilting in the heat of reality's flower…
the circle of my thoughts bearing east across
the vague splendor of a dying wind,
in grey autumnal words, the smoke of life drifting north,
over a world of sourceless crimes,
all things bearing right to the soul,
surviving disillusion.

Nigredo

I.

The night's dying black above below the voided spirit,
hungry beneath rapid solitudes,
memories, the slightest breeze tearing thought in two,
scattering, by turns, starlight ever-disappearing…
the eyes, the words angered,
silent, without beginning.

The night's dying in tumescent beauty,
tearing up the human root,
its morbid wreckage dying in the hands…
late the world in still burial, the horror of tranquilities,
shades of faces in masks, dehumanized & abstract,
the sleeping balance, the injured word,
the injured love.

II.

In feared silence,
the night caresses the wind,
blowing old miracles from my hands
as the last circle pours addiction in the stream,
the feared silence, the wind, the watch...

Fiercely,
in solid echoes of solitude,
the broken veins above my left eye,
within the trapped spirit of this stagnant peace,
exists the wind forming silences, uncertainties
& disillusion.

III.

Where in mystical refusal the cracked arena sits,
vague gestures are circles born,
stifled in afflicted shadows...
the waiting, the skies burning in rare futility,
with masculine grace,
the shadows fuse, wherein dangerous peril burns fictions
scarring the eye,
the lyric painting oblivion,
the shadow of motion posing in servile postures,
the sky of all existence.

Part IV.

Ergo

In the last hour of spiritual decay,
you will ask–what is the asking–as skies eagerly cross the gap,
plane to plane, in the last hour of spiritual decay,

In the black an open sky, then grey,
on the still beauty of your mouth, eyes glowing,
when skies have been created,
sipping eagerly the material beauty of your mouth,
eyes glowing, one plane to another...skies sipping eagerly your
material beauty...

In the last hour of spiritual decay,
the vague question that needs answering,
to touch once with glowing eyes the material beauty
of the world.

Aphoria

I.

This afternoon fuses to the eye
billowing light all but diminished,
tearing bit by bit the wind, the imagery,
black & white, in terrible afflictions, the pointless pointing
of man spilling redundancies, yet kept alive somehow
by the perseverance of this linguist's art.

This parallelism of surrealist diction & partialities,
the "it" too loud, the nerves too dense,
the sun too close to the abstract miracle
of this living motion.

II.

We watch the finished product
balance tranquilly between the cornea & image,
the day becoming that dying shadow I told you about,
except for the crying sun & broiling flesh,
the tears of sex & those lost the day finds crawling
to the next thought, bearing doves that fall white at my feet.

Their miracle no longer in place,
they speak in lyric pathologies,
murmuring death before the fact,
descending to the portion left & less miserable thoughts.

III.

Yesterday afternoon,
I was afraid spring passed the same point of being,
until centered on my forehead a miracle panted for sense,
the belly too hot, the word too close...
everything hard & poetic pulling this summer to earth,
the sun in green holding a vague air,
some absolute movement in tranquility,
beginning & ending metamorphoses,
suspecting tomorrow & vague breezes,
holding nothing but the beginning & end...

Some obscure smoke, white & lazy,
lifts off-shore, stagnant & still the alliteration of this line,
remembering redundancy, a sadly forgotten existence,
even my own.

IV.

Today the sea is perfect,
the sun, a diaphanous color of blue-striated clouds,
like white ribbons stationary beneath blue...
readjusting impressions, destroying imagery,
somewhere crossing over a line of prose
at some lessened state of being...

That which saves, neither material, medicinal, biologic,
or spiritual, rests in conscience as we watch
the body suffer, tenuous & tight,
the final break caressing us in turn, giving back being,
the sun swimming a failed transparency of light,
hitting the retina's morbid reason for light.

V.

I have to talk to the wound face-to-face,
shirking happiness, the body's ineffable chemistry,
separating life from death,
perforating the wound of familial voices
that can't be separated from the ineffable dilemma
impaled on dying leaves…

VI.

I listen to my heart heave & withdraw,
pursuing each breath's liberation between beats,
a number affixed forever.

Every minute, I realize the end in formless space,
between hope & dying…
the sun against my chest, a rolling sky over my throat,
slowly dropping words, spilling to earth,
the wind & translucent clouds…
time pressing the afternoon, having grown two reflections, imitating the sun.

VII.

There a burning blue light to my left,
breaking through sky & leaves, bathing morning,
clean of quietude...echoing the prayer summer revives,
we who think, awakened to the hammer,
needing need in knowing becomes need & art.

Dissolve the future's symmetry,
broken in prayer, leaving no sound...
the heart, a broken sphere passing overhead,
denuded white, sheltered blue, from blue to white,
white in transition.

VIII.

There dead silence weakly telling the night,
running beside sun & wind,
falling in vague shape & all barriers between.

Now the light, the leaves,
transparent in movement, the child preserved,
a vague shape falling between morning's transition,
in light burning tomorrow's circle,
in changing shape, my guitar's tearful dying,
empty inside the stomach of love.

Synoptic

There is something man cannot do,
bewildered or indifferent, inundated with the world,
joined by all wills, together in epiphany,
orchestrating, drop-by-drop, our bleeding,
enough to see faces tired in expectation…

Stupid as we are,
ignorant as we are, the earth bleeds at our feet,
fused & archaeologic,
flesh-to-flesh of others in burning rituals,
trying to speak man's last dying whisper,
addressing the obvious if he speaks,
& momentarily becomes eternal.

Paradox

The sound of daylight
& some dying having passed the demure hour,
daylight on the passage of leaves,
sweet in the passage of our mysteries,
deflects the minutes counted out of hand.

Sitting, waiting,
their shadows burn beyond recognition,
kisses restrained in the humid world
of my perception, walking calmly
to the victory of paradox.

The brothers of tears
falling through my shirt & humility before life,
quickening to a standstill.

Persona

My face devises a transcription,
telling it what to feel…a cleft pain touching each section,
a transforming cry of crawling encyclicals
through my words, even if the face appears,
the point still breaks & spills.

Isn't that what stops the courage,
reforms the mind?… wait!…the sun!…
that should crack idealism well in two,
straightening strategic lines of thought,
bearing the weight, my shoulder, dead on the table,
moving the shape of leaves.

Nocturne

I.

Vague sounds grow the night,
the canopy, the ineffable changing colors,
sink & pour effusive light over the trees,
still but for one or two windy hours,
& all the differences in the world resolve in realization,
the final breath, soundless against my face.

To keep the first step
that pours the light still moving,
languorous & light, silent, immobile, blue,
the worthless secret of my days climbing midday,
like buddhic wheels washing these hands in humility,
the dream in pain trying to reach the heart in pain,
trying to bleed.

II.

The light beams away,
falling to shadows, the last leaves burning…
the leaves, the death, the life, the sun's rough edges,
descending worlds of shade,
as the light dips ever softer against imminent night,
uncertainty, blue barely spoiled white,
savage & pure, tranquil & sad.

For all the kisses,
the savage light still pours white, savage & serene,
beyond burning, forgetting our savage grace
that takes us, one mind to another,
having no prayer, but to reality.

III.

Everything
diminishes to earth,
burning its way to skies momentarily black,
leaves scarcely living one second…muted, burning
in such burning, in ashes bleeding the human miracle
that transforms the first word nearer night,
forcing the sky's issue.

Bending, sleeping, swaying, the movement below night,
the final step, cutting branches, arms & wind,
sending message.

IV.

My minutes
pace diurnal mountains,
as winds race through these bleeding seconds,
one lives a grey-wasting perfection…
dismal grey without death,
but some facsimile descending, an oneiric stream
of cloud & essence.

Perhaps fatigue
is worth one savior's coat,
playing with these prepositions that do no
proposing, but sing more diurnal filaments of being
on the mouth of my pluralities,
aching against this touch.

V.

Savaging my right eye,
one sun sinking into a vacant cloud,
crying one sweet word washed in sunlight...
winter's seer cloud in my right eye,
seals my fate, a scattered sun burning air,
a black poem barking through my fingers self-consciously.

A black poem's sin sorting refuse,
a banished sound crumpled to the floor.

VI.

For a moment,
light freezes in place the last summer,
forming its image, the surface,
its diurnal white wing soiled,
surrendering my sight, becoming my mouth,
all voice, crying the fictions I see.

The wing white,
soiled, descending, light & somnolent,
in aloneness pouring some tired miracle through my veins,
inspiration crying to sleep these infinitives,
final & blue, shaping the night
right here behind this susceptible eye,
peering into fragments, metamorphoses, shadows,
behind words, obscure pains wrecking my soliloquies,
dying pensively in this savage minute.

Finis

The soft, falling, final snow,
final touch, final doubt, hidden under nights
pensively puerile, a paradox of puerile conceptions
that touch softly when I am not looking, when it all matters...
the poor substitute, the artificial light.

Who's to say
everything isn't finally buried in soft recline,
only waiting, the sweet lonely taste of being,
the vagaries of words & thought,
bearing great expense that finally touch,
breaking other form, final & unadulterated?

Doesn't the symptom force the issue,
not the conception you imagined of light,
showing the first sign of decay in the final light of experience,
that final, falling touch, light on dark,
nothing mattering, but light blazing uniform
against my cheek.